Scholastic Children's Books
Euston House,
24 Eversholt Street,
London NW1 1DB, UK

A division of Scholastic Ltd
London ~ New York ~ Toronto ~ Sydney ~ Auckland
Mexico City ~ New Delhi ~ Hong Kong

Written by Stephanie Clarkson
Line illustrations by Diana Hill
Produced for Scholastic by 38a The Shop

Published in the UK by Scholastic Ltd, 2015
© Scholastic Children's Books, 2015

ISBN 978 1407 16288 1

Printed and bound by Bell & Bain Ltd, United Kingdom

10 9 8 7 6 5

Papers used by Scholastic Children's Books are made
from woods grown in sustainable forests.

www.scholastic.co.uk

Vlog It!

YOUR TOP VLOGGERS RIGHT HERE!

SCHOLASTIC

CONTENTS

I ❤ VLOGGING

If you've only picked up this book because your parents are yelling at you to take a screen break, then welcome and well done – you've made a smart move. This is the ultimate guide to the world of vlogging! When you've finished reading all about this new online trend, have met its break-out stars, learned about vlogging styles and read up on facts and stats, you can log on and begin to apply your new-found knowledge. Who knows? You might be the next Zoella or Alfie Deyes...

DISCOVER...

- **The vlogging community.** Who's who and who knows who.

- **Vlog types.** From fashion and food, to music and travel – there are vlogs exploring every element of our lives.

- **Ones to watch.** Meet the upcoming stars.

- **Viral vids.** Funny, crazy clips viewed by millions.

- **Sensational stats.** Facts and quick quizzes to test your smarts.

- **How to get started.** Tips, ideas and invaluable advice from those in the know on creating your own vlog.

BE SMART

BE SAFE

This book is all about vlogging, connecting and having fun, but it's important to be responsible when you go online. Smart vloggers always check that they are cyber-safe. Here's how to make sure that you do the same.

ALWAYS:

- Check with a parent or guardian before you post content on the Internet. If you want to set up your own channel, get permission and agree the basic ground rules first.

- Check the rules and age limit of any website that you're planning to use and involve your parents in your plans. Don't upload footage if you're younger than the minimum age. If that means that you have to wait a while before you can start vlogging, don't panic. Use this time to work on your filming, presenting and editing skills. Practice makes perfect!

- Use common sense when viewing other people's vlogs. Although every effort has been made to recommend appropriate channels in this book, some stars still occasionally upload content that may not be suitable for you. Use your common sense and if you're unsure, talk to an adult about it.

NEVER:

- Give out details such as your address, phone number or date of birth.

- Post personal or offensive content. Once footage has been made public, you cannot control what others do with it. Clips could come back to haunt you at a later date. As a general rule, if you wouldn't be happy with your parent, guardian or teacher viewing your vlog post, don't upload it.

- Get into arguments with people online. If you can't say anything nice, don't post anything at all. If anyone is acting in a mean or threatening way towards you, log off then tell an adult that you trust what has happened.

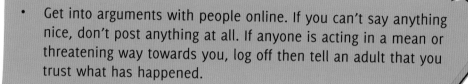

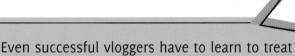

Even successful vloggers have to learn to treat the Internet with care. In the past Zoella has found herself the victim of cyber-bullying. In an interview she said, "I've had comments about my appearance, that I'm not a good role-model, that I lie about having anxiety just to get views. Pretty much anything you could think of, I've read. They wanted to upset me or make me feel rubbish and that's exactly what they did... It knocks your confidence a bit."

Zoella says this happens because, "It's very easy for somebody to type whatever they want to type, press send and [then not] even think about it." Her way of dealing with cyber-bulling is to ignore the negative attention and focus on the positive comments her fans make instead.

BRAVE **NEW** WORLD

Chances are that if you mention the word 'vlogging' to your parents (or anyone over the age of 30), they'll think you're talking about a medieval form of torture, but this 21st century phenomenon has revolutionized the way we communicate. Anyone who hasn't explored the world online is most definitely missing out. So what exactly is vlogging and how did it develop?

Vlog *noun*
A video log. A blog posted in video form.

Vlogger *noun*
An individual documenting their life, thoughts, opinions and interests in video form on the web.

One small vlog for Adam...

The origins of vlogging can be traced back to January 2000. Adam Kontras, who was moving to LA to pursue a career in show business, began posting video clips within the blog of his journey. The first clip lasted just 14 seconds. It showed him and his fiancée Jessica in the lift of their hotel in Springfield, Missouri, USA. Adam is still vlogging today and has become the longest running video blogger in the world.

Year of the vlog

In 2005 vlogging really arrived as a means of self-expression when an innovative new website called YouTube was created. The site allowed users to upload and share video content. Suddenly there was an explosion of people creating and watching vlogs – by 2006 an estimated 100 million videos were being watched daily. By 2009, YouTube was getting a billion visits per day.

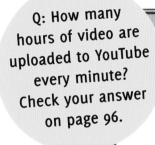

Q: How many hours of video are uploaded to YouTube every minute? Check your answer on page 96.

GET INSPIRED!

GET CREATIVE!

GET VLOGGING!

Vlog for all

Vlogging has continued to soar in popularity due to advances in technology, which means that anyone can easily shoot, upload and share video using a smartphone or tablet. These days vlogging is considered a proper medium, with its own community and celebrities. Vloggers use their films as video journals, to share information or as a way to express themselves in a direct and 'real' way. Logging on at home, we just love to watch, learn from, be entertained by and interact with our favourite vlogging stars!

Zoella

► *"Helloooo, everybody!"*

NAME:	Zoe Elizabeth Sugg
VLOGS AS:	ZOELLA and MoreZoella
DOB:	28/03/90
BORN:	Lacock, Wiltshire, UK
VLOGGING SINCE:	2009
FIRST VID:	60 Things In My Bedroom
SUBSCRIBERS:	Eight million and counting

Zoella loves...

Her guinea pigs and her pug, Nala, scented candles, fairy lights, chummy chats with her BFF Louise.

Never thought I'd be...

- photographed for *Vogue*
- a bestselling author
- launching my own beauty line

Zoe Sugg was always destined for online stardom. She recently unearthed an old home video where she talked her (at that point imaginary) viewers through the contents of her holiday suitcase. She was 11 years old. Fast forward a decade and Zoe is still in her bedroom, sharing her life, but these days there's nothing remotely imaginary about Zoe's viewers – she has over eight million subscribers to her YouTube channel. Zoe (or Zoella as she's now globally known) is widely adored for her approachable, enthusiastic 'big sister' persona. Queen of 'haul' videos – which involve her talking through recent purchases from high street stores like Primark and Top Shop – she has also branched into beauty and lifestyle. Zoe says her success is due to her being 'a normal girl' and despite her undeniable fame, believes her subscribers think of her as their friend rather than as a celebrity.

"I THINK IT'S SO AMAZING THAT SOMEONE IS ABLE TO PICK UP A CAMERA AND UPLOAD WHATEVER THEY WANT TO A FREE SOCIAL PLATFORM AS ENTERTAINMENT FOR OTHERS, OR FOR THEIR OWN PERSONAL REASONS."

shop

CONNECT WITH ZOELLA on...

Twitter @ZozeeBo; Instagram.com/zozeebo or via her website www.zoella.co.uk

HAUL OF FAME

Zoella is just one of the many YouTubers to embrace the amazingly popular 'haul' trend. A haul is the stash of things bought during a shopping spree.

Haul-ers are...

Happy, bubbly relatable types. They've got their eye on style trends, but they're not haughty fashionistas aiming to sit front row at London Fashion Week. They're just girls like you, who love shopping and are excited to share the joy of their new stuff – just as you would do if you'd just been on a shopping trip with your BFF.

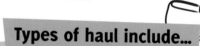

Types of haul include...

- **The seasonal haul**
  (shopping for a season such as Spring or Autumn.)

- **The holiday haul**
  (pre-Christmas or summer hols or January sales shopping.)

- **The one-stop shop haul**
  (a blow-out at a favourite high street or online store.)

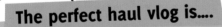

The perfect haul vlog is....

- **Like Christmas** – full of enticingly wrapped things in colourful carrier bags.

- **Informative** – you the viewer should get an idea of why the item shown is a 'must-have', with everything from price to quality of material discussed.

- **Brief** – there's only so long you can look at a lipstick. Overly lengthy vlogs where each item is shot from a million angles are a turn-off.

Get Mota-vated

The US's answer to Zoella, Bethany Noel Mota, from Los Banos, California, is a global phenomenon with over eight and a half million subscribers to her YouTube channel. Bethany posted her first haul vlog in 2009 and has since amassed an army of fans she calls her 'Mota-vators'. Bethany's vlogging has opened countless doors – she came fourth on the US version of *Strictly*, has her own clothing line, has released a single and has even interviewed US President Barack Obama.

Do vloggers actually buy the stuff they film?

Once a haul vlogger has a huge online presence, companies send them items in the hope that they'll talk about them on-screen. However, passing 'freebies' off as your own buys is a no-no and the quickest way to alienate you from your followers. Although haulers like Zoella and Bethany are courted by many companies, the savvy girls always make sure to state when they have purchased items themselves and when they are talking about a 'freebie' – which they only do when they will genuinely use or wear it.

TEN GREAT HAUL VLOGS

1. Zoe Sugg – Zoella
2. Bethany Mota – MacBarbie07
3. Blair Fowler – JuicyStar07
4. Elle Fowler – AllThatGlitters21
5. Asia – AllThingsFabulous101
6. Becca Rose – Becca Rose
7. Patricia Bright – Patricia Bright
8. Lily Melrose – Lily Melrose
9. Lily Pebbles – Lily Pebbles
10. Jessie – SunbeamsJess

DO GIVE UP THE DAY JOB

Are vloggers just people with nothing better to do, messing about in their bedrooms? They may well have started out that way, but many have turned a hobby into a full-time career. It's crazy what can be achieved if you follow your vlogging dreams!

Loose ends

We've all slouched around the house on a rainy Sunday, feeling bored. Successful vloggers use this downtime to get creative and go online. They begin by simply chatting to camera about things they like and, if their style is appealing and their content entertaining, viewers take note. Engaging with subscribers is the key to growing viewing figures and making money.

Rags to riches #1 – high roller

Charlie McDonnell, from Bath in Somerset, is the perfect example of someone whose hobby has transformed into a career. The self-confessed science nerd and musician began posting clips about stuff that he liked in 2007. After Oprah Winfrey played one of his clips called 'How To Be English' on her show, he became the first British YouTuber to hit a million regular views. His channel CharlieIsSoCoolLike boasts two and a half million subscribers. He now earns more than his parents.

Rags to riches #2 – home owner

At the age of just 24, Zoella has recently bought her first house. The queen bee's new pad is reportedly worth over a million pounds, boasting five en-suite bathrooms, a designer kitchen and a log cabin in the grounds. Not bad for a girl who just a few years ago was unemployed after quitting her job in interior design.

Rags to Riches #3 – globetrotter

In July 2013, Jack Harries decided to set up a vlog to keep his family up to date with his gap year travels with his twin Finn. Little did he know that JacksGap would become so popular that advertising revenue from YouTube would be funding his entire trip through Thailand. "I never expected that," he says. "I try to put most of the money into camera equipment, but if there's some left over to go on holiday and have fun, then why not?"

KERRRRCHIIIING!

So how does your vlog convert into cold hard cash? The key is advertising. Video makers can earn money via the YouTube partner programme, a scheme aimed at regular uploaders with big audiences. You share in the money generated when people watch your clips.

As a partner you must agree to YouTube allowing adverts to be placed alongside or within your clips. You then earn money based on a combination of the 'impressions' (views) and 'clicks' (how many people click on the ad) that the clip receives. Adverts that appear 'pre-roll' (ie before your clip begins playing) earn the most dosh.

Anyone can apply to be a partner as long as they regularly upload original videos that are viewed by thousands of people, and either own, or have permission to use, all the audio and video content. Amazingly, YouTube's technology can even predict when a video is about to be huge and then contact you about advertising, so that you can make money from just one clip going viral.

How much can top vloggers charge?

Up to **£20,000** per month for banners and 'skins' around the edges of web pages.

Up to **£4,000** per mention of a product.

Up to **£4,000** per Instagram or Twitter post featuring the product.

Up to **£10,000** per personal appearance.

It's not just about the money, money, money

Making an income from doing something you love is a big bonus, but the focus has to be on the videos. Forget this and your audience (and cash flow) will quickly dry up. British beauty vlogger Lily Pebbles says...

"I DON'T THINK WE SHOULD BE ASHAMED OF HOW MUCH MONEY WE'RE EARNING. IT'S JUST IMPORTANT PEOPLE KNOW THE MONEY DOESN'T AFFECT HOW WE WRITE OUR WEBSITES."

THE FAME GAME

Besides bringing in the bacon, vlogging can open other exciting doors. From modelling opportunities to book deals, clothing lines to red carpet invites, glitz and glamour are never far away...

Sophie Merry (BandyToaster), known for her 'Groovy Dancing Girl' clips on YouTube, was invited to star in a jeans campaign for French clothing label Etam. She was overwhelmed to be flown to Paris and given the VIP treatment. "It's like I'm a movie star," she said on the set of her modelling shoot.

Louise Pentland (SprinkleOfGlitter) was just one of the British YouTubers invited to the world première of One Direction's movie *This Is Us*. "That's definitely one of the best moments of my life... a life highlight!" she gasped from the red carpet, before thanking the fans of her vlog for making it possible.

Alfie Deyes (PointlessBlog) has had two books published, *The Pointless Book* and *The Pointless Book 2*, something he never would have thought possible. "Look, it's like a proper book... the real thing guys, I've got my own book. This is insane... I designed, I literally planned every single page of this book. It is for sale. How mad is that?" he cried excitedly when showing off his advance copies.

Tyler Oakley (Tyler Oakley) has schmoozed with some of the most famous people on the planet. The US vlogger has interviewed Michelle Obama about her higher education initiative 'Reach Higher', chatted to Ed Sheeran and had a good old chinwag with friend and *Modern Family* actor, Jesse Tyler Ferguson. Despite his celeb pals, he still gets starstruck. On finding that Harry Styles had retweeted him, he exclaimed, "He called me mate! I am freaking out!"

#STARSTRUCK

Tanya Burr (Tanya Burr) has moved from trialling established make-up lines to releasing her own. On the launch of Tanya Burr Cosmetics she said, "I'm so, so excited to be releasing my own product line. I've started small with lip glosses and nail polish just because I feel I'm really passionate about those products in particular. The thing about the range is that it's all my favourite colours, named after all of my favourite things."

Q: Can you match the vlogger with their pre-fame activities?

1 Being an extra in *Harry Potter And The Philosopher's Stone*.

2 Training as an apprentice roof thatcher.

3 Exhibiting work at an art gallery.

4 Working in Disney World, Florida.

5 Working at Topshop.

6 Interning at a celebrity PR firm.

7 Working 9–5 in an office.

8 Working in insurance.

a PewDiePie

b MirandaSings

c ThatcherJoe

d SprinkleOfGlitter

e Zoella

f Tyler Oakley

g Jim Chapman

h Tanya Burr

The answers are on page 96!

TANYA BURR

▶ *"Hey guys!"*

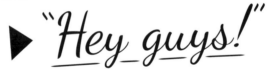

NAME:	Tanya Burr
VLOGS AS:	Tanya Burr
DOB:	28/03/90
BORN:	Norwich, Norfolk UK
VLOGGING SINCE:	2009
FIRST VID:	Serena (*Gossip Girl*'s Blake Lively) make-up tutorial
SUBSCRIBERS:	Just under three million

Never thought I'd be...

- releasing my own cosmetics line
- on the judging panel for the Elle Beauty Awards
- publishing my diary in pictures on the *Grazia Daily* website

Tanya loves...

A cosy onesie, perfect pedicures, baking, holidays with the girls, her fiancé Jim.

If Zoella is the vlogging queen of haul, Tanya Burr is the princess of beauty. After asking for advice from make-up artist friend Sam Chapman, whose brother Jim she was dating, Tanya did a short course as a make-up artist then earned her beauty stripes working in-store on make-up counters for big brands like Laura Mercier and Clinique. For a while she modelled for Sam and Nic Chapman's Pixiwoo online make-up tutorials and then, having gained in confidence, she began vlogging in 2009. Tanya's make-up tutorials follow celeb trends. She can help you replicate Cara Delevigne's smokey-eyed Burberry ad look one week and Kylie Jenner's fresh-yet polished style the next. Fans love the way Tanya responds to their specific requests, producing content to suit their needs, such as showing them specific products to deal with teen skin breakouts. Tanya is soon to be married to long-term love and fiancé Jim Chapman.

"YOUTUBE IS SO REAL... [REALITY TV] IS NOT AS REAL AS YOU THINK IT IS. WHEREAS, WHEN I VLOG, IT'S COMPLETELY REAL. PEOPLE ARE JUST SEEING MY LIFE."

CONNECT WITH TANYA on...

Twitter @TanyaBurr; instagram.com/tanyaburr or via her website www.tanyaburr.co.uk

BEAUTY AND THE BEST

Camera, camera on the wall, who's the best beauty vlogger of them all? It's not just Tanya – many are vying to claim this title as their own.

Types of beauty vlog include...

- **How-to make-up tutorials**
  Step-by-steps to achieving the basics.

- **Celebrity make-up tutorials**
  How to channel a celebrity's signature look.

- **Extreme make-up tutorials**
  Learn to create incredible effects for parties or Halloween.

The perfect beauty vlog is...

- **Well lit** – if the vlogger isn't using natural light or professional studio lighting how will you see the results of their work?

- **Varied** – using a mix of products that you can afford or save up for.

- **Encouraging** – showing how anyone can work to make the best of what they've got.

Visit Vivianna

When it comes to make-up vlogs, British girls are blazing a trail. Anna Gardner has been posting as ViviannaDoesMakeup since 2011. She was inspired to start vlogging while searching online for a 1940s make-up look. Her vlog name (prefixing her name with 'Vivi') was an attempt to disguise herself from people she knew. Anna needn't have worried however, she has 300,000 subscribers to her channel and around 1.4 million views per month. Anna gets ideas from people watching and believes great skincare is as vital as clever make-up.

Are all beauty vloggers professional make-up artists?

Some vloggers like Lisa Eldridge and Sam Chapman (Pixiwoo) are professional make-up artists turned vloggers, but many are just every day people with a penchant for powder and a love of lipstick. Some, including Anna Gardner and Tanya Burr, have worked on beauty counters. Most are self-taught, combining their passion for make-up with a great presenting style.

TEN GREAT BEAUTY VLOGS

1. Tanya Burr – Tanya Burr
2. Sam and Nic Chapman – Pixiwoo
3. Lisa Eldridge – Lisa Eldridge
4. Michelle Phan – Michelle Phan
5. Suzie Bonaldi – Hello October
6. Louise Pentland – SprinkleOfGlitter
7. Sandi Ball – CutePolish
8. Anna Gardner – Vivianna Does Make-Up
9. Ruth Crilly – A Model Recommends
10. Andrea Brooks – Andrea's Choice

JIM CHAPMAN

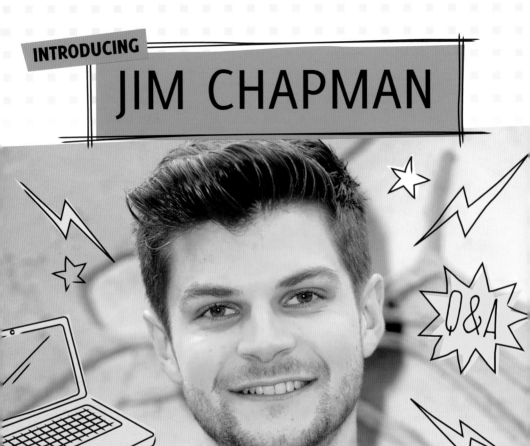

▶ *"Hello best friends!"*

NAME:	James Alfred Chapman
VLOGS AS:	Jim Chapman
DOB:	28/12/87
BORN:	Norwich, Norfolk UK
VLOGGING SINCE:	2009
FIRST VID:	My Rules For Camping (festival-ing)
SUBSCRIBERS:	Two million and counting

Never thought I'd be...

- co-presenting ITV2 show *Viral Tap* with Caroline Flack
- being shot by *GQ Magazine*
- hosting the Mockingjay live event for *The Hunger Games* with Alex Zane

Jim loves...

Twin John and big sisters Sam and Nic, New York, classic tailoring by British brands, 'man-crush' Brad Pitt, burgers with bacon and avocado, first love turned fiancée Tanya.

Tall, affable and energetic, Jim Chapman makes vlogging look easy, but then he took tips from the very best. Jim's elder sisters Sam and Nic (the duo behind Pixiwoo) and fiancée Tanya Burr are all at the top of their game and (luckily for us) they encouraged Jim to put himself out there, too. Jim studied psychology at university, and was working in the insurance and retail sectors when he first began posting clips. He started posting in earnest following time out travelling, and says that it was only when he began vlogging from the heart that people started taking notice. Jim's vlogs are extremely varied. One day he'll be trying out male grooming products and another he'll be baking cake-pops! His 'Ask Jim/Dare Jim' clips, where he responds to fan's queries and ideas, are extremely popular, as are his 'Awful Advice' clips where he talks about everything from surviving high school to dating girls.

"MY AUDIENCE WILL WATCH ME AS LONG AS I RESPECT THEM AND I AM DOING THE THINGS THEY WANT ME TO DO."

CONNECT WITH JIM on...

Twitter @JimsTweetings; instagram.com/jimstweetings or via his website www.jimchapman.co.uk

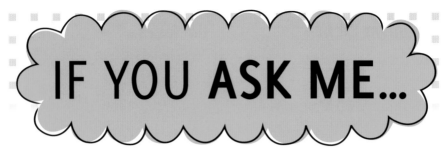

IF YOU ASK ME...

We all get lonely or low sometimes. If you feel you've got no one to turn to, switch on your computer or tablet instead. You'll find a whole host of virtual shoulders to cry on, as well as helpful advice and reassurance.

Types of advice include...

- **Back to school**
  How to cope with new teachers, new terms, homework and other trials.

- **Self-confidence**
  How to learn to love yourself inside and out.

- **Dating**
  How to deal with boyfriends and girlfriends, from friendships to crushes and first dates.

The perfect advice vlog is...

- **Personal** – the vlogger ideally needs to have some personal experience of the issue they're discussing to be able to offer advice.

- **Amusing** – sometimes the way to overcome an issue is to learn to laugh at it.

- **Chatty** – although the content is serious, there's no need for the tone to be. Fans appreciate seeing their vloggers' usual, relatable presenting style.

SprinkleOfGlitter

"Aloha Sprinklerinos!" Bubbly Louise Pentland began her vlogging career focusing on beauty and shopping, but her empathetic, girl-next-door persona meant viewers wanted more. In response to chat among her fans, Louise began making videos on big topics including body confidence, religion and the quest for happiness. Louise grew up in Northampton, England and is mum to daughter Darcy AKA Baby Glitter from her marriage to Matt Watson. She has a spin-off channel called SprinkleOfChatter where she uploads lifestyle vlogs including 'Chummy Chatter' clips with BFF Zoella.

Do vloggers really have all the answers?

No. They definitely do not. Vloggers offer advice on serious topics such as eating disorders, anxiety and bullying but it is important to remember that they are not (in the majority of cases) qualified psychiatrists or psychotherapists. What vloggers can do is relate to some of the issues you may be going through as a teen, tween or young adult. Hearing their thoughts and experiences may help you to feel less isolated, motivate you to take positive steps or even seek professional help.

TEN GREAT ADVICE VLOGS

1. Jim Chapman – Jim Chapman
2. Louise Pentland – SprinkleOfGlitter
3. Marcus Butler – Marcus Butler
4. Jenna Mourey – Jenna Marbles
5. Dan Howell – DanIsNotOnFire
6. Phil Lester – Amazing Phil
7. Nikki Phillippi – Nikki Phillippi
8. Meghan Rienks – Meghan Rienks
9. Lauren Curtis – Lauren Curtis
10. Zoe Sugg – Zoella

CHALLENGE VLOGGER

Vloggers are daring types! They're quick to set and accept all kinds of crazy challenges, many of which become web-wide trends. Check out some of the most popular. Are you up to the test?

The 'yoga' challenge

Grab a friend and attempt to recreate some acrobatic yoga poses. Double downward dog anyone?

The 'not my arms' challenge

Prepare to look terrible as you get ready using someone else's arms, while yours remain tucked behind your back.

The 'blindfolded make-up' challenge

Do exactly that. Take it in turns to apply make-up to your friend while wearing a blindfold. Pretty!

The 'try not to laugh' challenge

The aim is to make your opponent, who has a mouth full of water, laugh any way you can within 30 seconds.

The 'dizzy' challenge

You'll need an office chair to spin around on before you try to attempt basic tasks without careering off balance. Warning: can get messy and you may die laughing.

AUSTRALIAN

The 'accent' challenge

Write down different accents from Australian to Essex. Take turns picking them out, talking in that accent and trying to get your opponent to correctly guess which one you're doing.

It's all for charidee...

Some challenges have gone viral and made millions. Vlogger Sawyer Hartman has an entire thread of clips called 'Challenges For Charity', where he invites fellow YouTubers to undertake challenges and quizzes to raise money for their chosen good causes.

The Ice Bucket Challenge, raising money for Motor Neurone sufferers, was an Internet sensation. It involved having a bucket of cold, ice-filled water thrown over a person's head. Victims then nominated friends to take up the challenge. Freezing but very, very funny.

Q: Who is getting icily soaked in this pic? Check your answer on page 96.

INTRODUCING MIRANDA SINGS

▶ "Hey guys, it's me *Miranda*."

NAME:	Colleen Ballinger
VLOGS AS:	Miranda Sings
DOB:	21/11/86
BORN:	Santa Barbara, California, USA
VLOGGING SINCE:	2007
FIRST VID:	Miranda singing *White Christmas*
SUBSCRIBERS:	Just over four million

Never thought I'd be...

- in a car getting coffee with comedian Jerry Seinfeld
- touring with my one-woman Miranda show
- popping up on my magician brother Chris's vlogs

Miranda loves...

Her fans (Mirfandas), red sweat pants (with 'haters back off' on the booty) her vlogging BAEs, trademark red lipstick, applied super-perfectly.

Classically-trained singer Colleen Ballinger first began vlogging via her YouTube channel 'Psychosoprano' as a way to upload her performances from college where she was a singing student. The character Miranda was born from Colleen's experiences at college – she came across obnoxious, self-obsessed girls who posted terrible clips of themselves online, thinking they'd soon become famous. Colleen initially only posted the clips of Miranda as an in-joke between herself and her friends. However people loved to hate the delusional and tone-deaf character and the hits to the MirandaSings channel were soon mounting. A clip called 'Free Voice Lessons' in which Miranda gives singing tips, got almost a million views. Colleen says her aim was to get people (Miranda calls them 'haters') to post rude comments. She then responded to these by exaggerating Miranda's worst and most irritating characteristics. Typical Miranda vlogs include outrageously bad covers of pop songs, terrible make-up tutorials and hilarious anti-hater rants.

"MY VIEWERS ARE MY BOSSES, SO IF THEY AREN'T HAPPY, I'M OUT OF A JOB."

CONNECT WITH MIRANDA on...

Twitter @MirandaSings; instagram.com/mirandasingsofficial or via her website mirandasings.com

ALL ABOUT ME

If you don't like to share information about yourself, then vlogging is definitely not for you! Vloggers love to open up on camera, creating an atmosphere of intimacy and friendship between themselves and their fans. Here are just some of the ways that they do it...

Meme *noun*
An activity, concept or catchphrase that spreads as a craze from person to person via the Internet.

Draw my life

This meme became popular in 2013. It involves producing a visual retrospective of your life – a bit like an autobiographical game of Pictionary! Simple to film, these vlogs

always feature a whiteboard and pen, focussing on the artist's hands as they draw and erase the illustrations. Results depend on the artistic skill of the vlogger, which can range from basic to brilliant. Some sneaky vloggers supply the voiceover, but draft someone else in to do the art.

Room tours

Particularly popular with tweens and teens, this meme features a vlogger showing the viewer around their room and pointing out items of interest. Sometimes they highlight particular ornaments that hold sentimental value or talk you through their wardrobe. As well as getting a tantalising glimpse of someone else's house, viewers can pick up hints and tips on storage, organization and interior design.

Morning and night routines

This meme verges on oversharing! These clips detail every element of the vlogger's routine at the start or the end of the day, from their bathroom regime, to fashion or food choices. Some vloggers produce special clips to deal with school days or weekends,

while others find the whole thing ridiculous. Caspar Lee's parody features him accidentally spraying himself in the eyes with hairspray, eating cold pizza for breakfast and dressing in a parade of animal onesies.

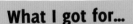

Sibling tags

Tags feature the vlogger and someone dear to them such as a brother, sister, BFF or roommate, answering a set of questions. These are usually compiled from ones that have been floating around the Internet and others posed by fans. The key to producing a successful tag is not just answering the questions honestly, but showing playful interaction between you both.

What I got for...

Want to remind yourself (and everyone else) how lucky you are at Christmas or on your birthday? This vlog clip allows you to display and talk through your haul of pressies. Vloggers have to work hard not to come across as spoiled or smug, but it's a good (if lazy) way of saying a collective 'thank you'.

Unscramble the letters to find the name of the YouTuber who regularly does sibling tag vlogs with his sister Skylynn.

The answer is on page 96!

GRAN RiESH ⟹ _ _ _ _ _ _ _ _ _ _

35

FUNNY GUYS

If your school report reads 'class clown' then filming your own vlog could be the perfect outlet for your antics! Thousands of vloggers use the Internet as a way to showcase their comedic talents. Why not join them?

Types of comedy vlog include...

- **Stand-up real talk**
  Funny takes on topics we can all relate to.

- **Skits and sketches**
  Dressing up, pretending, parodies and general mickey-taking. Who needs TV sketch shows?

- **Goofing off**
  Tripping, slipping, spilling stuff. There's humour in pretty much anything, guys! You'll find it all online.

Ha! Ha! HA! HA! *HA! HA!*

The perfect funny vlog is...

- **Well rehearsed** – or not. If you're delivering a monologue or sketch you'll want to practise, but there's a reason why the funniest clips are the out-takes.

- **Original** – whatever you do, you need to make it your own.

- **Accent heavy or pet based** – who doesn't love a great celeb impression or a cat attacking its own reflection?

Dan 'n' Phil

Need a quick pick-me-up after a bad day? Look no further than the hilarious YouTube musings of Dan Howell and Phil Lester. Encouraged by friends to upload videos, the pair have since amassed millions of subscribers to their channels DanIsNotOnFire and Amazing Phil. While Dan is self-effacing, his channel trailer begins with the words, "Hi Internet, I let you laugh at my life, so you can feel better about yours!", Phil's style is milder and more slapstick. His clips include, 'I Got Attacked By A Squirrel' and 'Stop Looking At My Spot.' The vloggers collaborate so often you'd be forgiven for thinking they're related, especially as they look so similar. They now even have their own show on BBC Radio 1.

Can anyone be funny?

Luckily because humour is such a personal thing, you'll pretty much always be funny to someone, somewhere. With its global reach, the Internet is the best way to find that someone – AKA your fanbase. Whether you set out to be funny or not, you'll soon be able to find out whether you have the comic skills necessary to make it.

TEN GREAT COMEDY VLOGS

1. Colleen Ballinger – Miranda Sings
2. Lex Croucher – TyrannosaurusLexx
3. Natalie Tran – Community Channel
4. Hazel Hayes – Chewing Sand
5. Ian Andrew Hecox and Anthony Padilla – Smosh
6. Christopher Bingham – Slomozovo
7. Lilly Singh – SuperWoman
8. Chris Kendall – CrabStickz
9. Caspar Lee – Caspar Lee
10. Grace Helbig – Grace Helbig

VFFs

FYI, that's vlogging friends forever! Vloggers are a sociable bunch and they've created a buzzing community, particularly in the UK. If these guys aren't house sharing, or getting hitched, they're hitting the shops or hanging out together. Take a look at the vlogging family tree...

TANYA BURR

JOE SUGG

SIBLINGS

FRIENDS

NIOMI SMART

FRIENDS

ZOE SUGG

ZALFIE!

DATING

NARCUS!

DATING

MARCUS BUTLER

FRIENDS

ALFIE DEYES

MALFIE!

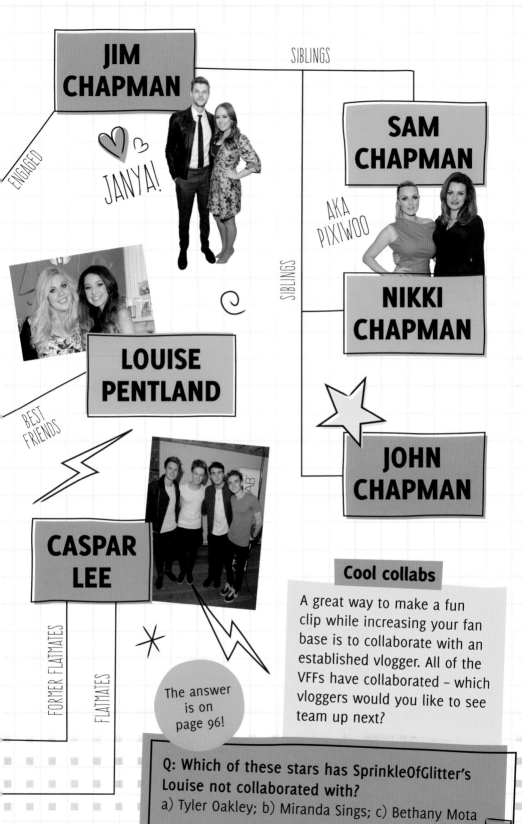

JIM CHAPMAN

SIBLINGS

SAM CHAPMAN

AKA PIXIWOO

NIKKI CHAPMAN

ENGAGED

JANYA!

SIBLINGS

LOUISE PENTLAND

JOHN CHAPMAN

BEST FRIENDS

CASPAR LEE

FORMER FLATMATES

FLATMATES

The answer is on page 96!

Cool collabs

A great way to make a fun clip while increasing your fan base is to collaborate with an established vlogger. All of the VFFs have collaborated – which vloggers would you like to see team up next?

Q: Which of these stars has SprinkleOfGlitter's Louise not collaborated with?
a) Tyler Oakley; b) Miranda Sings; c) Bethany Mota

GOT GAME?

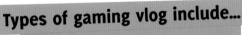

Chances are if you're not gaming, you love watching other people game. Gaming vlogs are packed with news on the latest releases, reviews and tips. To front this kind of vlog it's not enough just to be a great player. You also have to have brilliant delivery and an inexhaustible supply of killer quips.

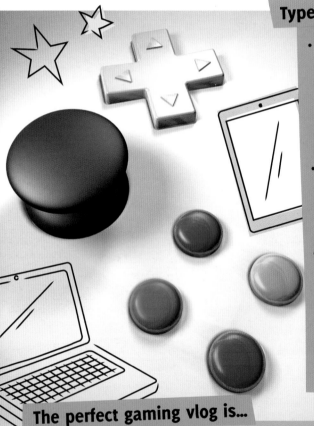

Types of gaming vlog include...

- **Walkthroughs**
  The vlogger plays the game and explains each element, walking you through the experience as if you were playing yourself.

- **Reviews**
  Detailing game-play, story campaigns and hidden content.

- **Vlogger-centric**
  These clips have the vloggers at their heart as much as the game itself. Fans love the vloggers' comments, reactions and game-related humour.

The perfect gaming vlog is...

- **Trailblazing** – previewing never-before-seen games and multiple uploads every week.

- **Action packed** – whether its racing, fighting, sports or adventure, fans respond to excitement, movement and sound.

- **Based on in-game footage** – not the high-def clips shown on the ads.

Shrewd Pewds

Born in Sweden, Felix Kjellberg AKA PewDiePie is YouTube's most famous vlogger. He has the power to make or break a new indie game, is developing his own game and even appeared as a cameo in *South Park*. Felix launched his own channel in 2010 with his 'Let's Play' videos. Pewd's USP is his funny reactions to game-play. He currently gains subscribers at an average of one per minute! Pewd understands that his success is largely down to his relationship with his viewers. He calls them his 'bros' rather than his fans, not wanting to feel removed from them. Felix now lives in Brighton with his vlogger girlfriend, Marzia.

Q: Where did the name PewDiePie come from?

Check your answer on page 96.

Stampede for Stampy

Not heard of Stampy? Get with the gaming programme! Joseph Garrett (aka 'Stampy' or confusingly 'Mr Stampy Cat') uploads at least one new video every single day and collects subscribers to his channels StampyLonghead, StampyLongnose and the brand new Wonder Quest, like others collect, well, stamps. Stampy is loved worldwide for his family friendly and action packed Minecraft-based gaming series.

TEN GREAT GAMING VLOGS

1. Felix Kjellberg – PewDiePie
2. Joseph Garrett – Stampy
3. Freddie Wong – FreddieW
4. Lewis Brindley and Simon Lane – Yogscast
5. Evan Frong – VanossGaming
6. James Richard Wilson Jr – UberHaxorNova
7. Charlotte Dyer – Master Char
8. Toby Turner – Tobuscus
9. Chris Dixon – Chris MD
10. Simon Minter – MiniMinter

TYLER OAKLEY

#FABULOSITY

#FANGIRL

Q & SLAY

▶ "*My name is Tyler Oakley...*"

NAME:	Tyler Oakley
VLOGS AS:	Tyler Oakley
DOB:	22/03/89
BORN:	Jackson, Michigan, USA
VLOGGING SINCE:	2007
FIRST VID:	Raindrops. Featuring Tyler talking from his college room
SUBSCRIBERS:	Over seven million

Never thought I'd be…

- the subject of a PBS documentary called *Generation Like*
- posting a GRAMMY live stream
- attending the SuperBowl as Pepsi's special guest

Tyler loves…

One Direction, bright hair dye, hula hooping, Zoella (he describes her as an infectiously positive human), making a difference with his charity work.

With his brightly-dyed hair, sweet smile and disarming lisp, Tyler Oakley is a huge vlogging personality. He began posting clips on YouTube at the age of 18 while studying at university. His first attempt was a simple greeting card to a bunch of friends that got around 100 views, but after a few more tries, the number of views had hit the millions. Tyler uploads two videos a week to his channel, mainly discussing pop music and describing what he's been up to. He also opens fan mail and responds directly to viewers' questions. He uses his YouTube fame channel and his fame as a platform to raise awareness about issues that he believes in. You'll find him talking about everything from standing up to bullies and 'being your special self' to the importance of education and the right to good health care.

"MY REACH COMES WITH A LOT OF RESPONSIBILITY AND IT'S SOMETHING THAT I TAKE VERY SERIOUSLY."

CONNECT WITH Tyler on…

Twitter @Tyleroakley; instagram.com/tyleroakley or via his website tyleroakley.com

43

LOUD AND PROUD

Vlogs can be a great way to raise awareness about the things that matter to you. These vloggers have all stood up to be counted...

Global hunger

Charlie McDonnell has worked with Unicef as well as other international charities. In 2013, he travelled to Tanzania with Save The Children to launch their #IFYouTube social media campaign working towards an end for world hunger.

Grief

Thomas Ridgewell AKA TomSka talked in detail about his friend and YouTube partner's Edd's cancer and death. Using his secondary channel, DarkSquidge, he posts clips such as 'Hellbound Promises', 'My

Friend Died' and 'Edd's Birthday', that focus on coping with grief and moving on.

Rights

Many vloggers like Jamie Pine and Tyler Oakley use their channels to stand up for gay rights.

Disability

UK based Mandeville Sisters (Amelia and Grace) have a 42,000-strong fanbase. They are currently taking YouTube by storm with their direct and fresh videos. Grace, the eldest, was born with one foreshortened arm and only one hand. The pair pepper sibling tags and other vlogging staples with posts about Grace's condition as well as the challenges and joys of prosthetics.

Mental illness

Anxiety can be crippling, in some cases confining the sufferer to his or home. That was certainly Zoella's experience. She and others among the YouTube community are keen to get the issue of mental health out in the open. Zoella is currently digital ambassador for the mental health charity MIND, spearheading their #DontPanicButton campaign.

Education

The Taco Bell Foundation for teens raises awareness of the high school dropout crisis. Tyler Oakley joined them to connect with young people and offer inspiration during their journey to educational success.

Bullying

Bullying affects thousands of young people. No wonder so many vloggers use their channels as a way to talk about the problems they have faced themselves. Vloggers who were once bullied include Ryan Higa, Colleen Ballinger, Lauren Curtis and Marcus Butler, to name but a few.

Homelessness

Louis Cole has done a lot to raise awareness for the homeless and for disadvantaged children. In 2007 he started the Boombus project, buying a double decker bus and equipping it as a music and gaming centre to help homeless youths.

Learning disabilities

US YouTuber Joey Graceffa had learning disabilities caused by ingesting lead paint on toys when he was a tot. He has been very vocal about his experiences at school where he was in special education classes until Year 7.

COMPLETELY CREATIVE

If you're a crafty type, the Internet is a fantastic way for you to share your skills or pick up new ones. There are vlogs on painting, doodling, knitting, baking, extreme make-up and any other craft you care to mention.

Here's where to look if you're feeling creative...

Art

For tips on anything from watercolours, to cartoon-style doodles visit...
- Lena Danya
- Mary Doodles
- Doodlekat1

Knitting

Woollen it be nice to knit yourself some new stuff? Try...
- KnitFitch
- JunkYarn
- Little Bobbins Knits

DIY

Looking for ways to cosy up your crib, paper your parlour or revamp your closet? These girls have tons of decorating and DIY ideas...
- MayBaby
- MyLifeAsEva

Baking

Got a sugar addiction? Feed it with wonderful sponges and cupcakes from...
- Rosanna Pansino – Nerdy Nummies
- My Cupcake Addiction
- Cupcake Jemma

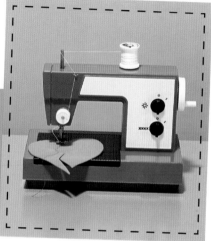

Sewing and much more

For an introduction to a whole range of crafting techniques (from crochet to quilting), visit...
- Violet V-Logs
- Melanie Ham

Food and healthy eating

You've gotta eat, right? Let these girls guide you round the kitchen, with one eye on top taste and the other on healthy eating habits...
- Cherry Wallis – Cherry's Kitchen
- Niomi Smart

Extreme make-up

If you want to learn how to create amazing looks that wouldn't be out of place on the big screen, there's only one place to go...
- KlaireDeLysArt

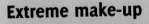

POINTLESS BLOG

▶ "What's up, guys!"

NAME:	Alfie Deyes
VLOGS AS:	Pointless Blog
DOB:	17/09/93
BORN:	London, UK
VLOGGING SINCE:	2009
FIRST VID:	Is Charlie So Cool Like?
SUBSCRIBERS:	Over four million

MY BOOK

Never thought I'd be...

- getting my make-up done by Ariana Grande
- mobbed by 8,000 fans at Waterstones for my book signing
- seeing my waxwork in Madame Tussauds

Alfie loves...

Breaking Guinness World Records, man-sturiser and other male grooming products, snacking from the fridge, Brighton, pal Marcus Butler, holidays in Greece and Dubai.

One half of YouTube power couple 'Zalfie' (with girlfriend Zoella – keep up!), Alfie's passion for the new medium has helped get him to the top of the vlogging world. The lovable lad has been a fan of YouTube since his early tweens. He used to beg his dad to take him to early events to meet vloggers he admired, such as the Shaytards and Rhett and Link. In 2009 he began posting his own clips based on the vaguely pointless, random stuff he loves doing, quickly discovering that he had a fan base. Alfie's loyal followers adore watching his onscreen antics, which are always random and incredibly varied. They include solving a Rubik's Cube in 30 seconds or 'fessing up about things that confuse him in life. Alfie's vlog has opened untold doors for him – he recently made Debrett's 500 most influential people in Britain list. Not bad for a boy who smells body parts and eats baby food for a living!

"I'VE ALWAYS LOVED THE INTERACTION AND THE OPPORTUNITY TO GET TO KNOW SOMEONE THROUGH THE INTERNET THAT YOU WOULDN'T GET TO KNOW WITHOUT IT."

CONNECT WITH ALFIE on...

Twitter @PointlessBlog; instagram.com/pointlessblog or via Facebook www.facebook.com/alfiedeyespointlessblog

Band Of ONLINE BROTHERS

Move over One Direction, we're crushing on a new group of handsome, talented lads and this time the appreciation's mutual. These boys want to hang out with us, they love chatting to us and sharing their news and their lives – hey, they even invite us (virtually) into their homes.

So who is it exactly that we've fallen for? Are these mystery guys singers, TV presenters, film stars? No, no and no again! In fact, a posse of ordinary boys-next-door turned big-time vloggers has grabbed our attention.

It's a twin thing...

Let's face it, two engaging vlogging bros are always better than one!

TWIN-FORMATION

Names:
Jack and Finn Harries

DOB:
13/05/93

Vlog as:
JacksGap

Guess what?
Their grandfather is the famous playwright Michael Frayn. Jack once had a bit part in an advert for KFC.

Q: What are Jack and Finn's full names?

TWIN-FORMATION

Names:
Niki and Sammy Albon

DOB:
20/02/92

Vlog as:
NikiNSammy

Guess what?
The boys shed a combined 16 stone while they were at university.

Q: Which famous county is home to these twins?

TWIN-FORMATION

Names:
Austin and Aaron Rhodes

DOB:
20/02/92

Vlog as:
TheRhodesBros

Guess what?
The boys were born in Ohio, but now live in Los Angeles.

Q: Which Ed Sheeran song did Aaron Rhodes famously film himself singing?

Q: How many of these cute and cool vloggers do you follow? Can you name them?

All of the answers are on page 96

Laptop ☆ camera ACTION!

Vlogs are, by nature, short films. Many YouTube stars have proved themselves to be both talented directors and producers, turning their clips into an art form.

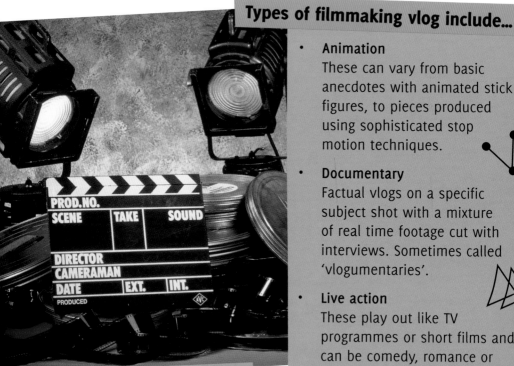

Types of filmmaking vlog include...

- **Animation**
  These can vary from basic anecdotes with animated stick figures, to pieces produced using sophisticated stop motion techniques.

- **Documentary**
  Factual vlogs on a specific subject shot with a mixture of real time footage cut with interviews. Sometimes called 'vlogumentaries'.

- **Live action**
  These play out like TV programmes or short films and can be comedy, romance or action based.

The perfect film vlog is...

- **Slick** – the animating techniques can be basic, but blurry shots or shaky camera angles are a no-no.

- **Innovative** – whichever style you're using, you need to make it fresh and exciting.

- **Multi-platform** – you don't have to limit yourself to YouTube. Skilled video content creators producing independent work use sites like Vimeo or BlipTV.

TomSka

Thomas Ridgewell began making short films as a child, using his parents' video camera. Little did he know that it would lead to a career in digital media! Now known by his vlogging name TomSka, Thomas is a full-time filmmaker whose animated creations asdfmovie and TurboPunch are enjoyed all over the world. Tom is also now at the helm of 'Eddsworld', the cartoon series he co-created with his friend Edd Gould (who died of cancer in 2012) and Matt Hargreaves. Besides his flair for animation, TomSka's unflinching honesty in the face of battles with weight, depression and grief set him apart, endearing him to his massive fanbase.

Q: What is the name of the film about vloggers shot by writer/director Benjamin Cook of NineBrassMonkeys?

Check your answer on page 96.

7

9

TEN GREAT FILM VLOGS

1. Thomas Ridgewell – TomSka
2. Benjamin Cook – NineBrassMonkeys
3. Benny and Rafi Fine – TheFineBros
4. Chris Trott, Ross Hornby and Alex Smith – HatFilms
5. Christopher Bingham – Slomovozo
6. John Patrick Douglass – JacksFilms
7. Toby Turner – Tobuscus
8. Corey Vidal – Vlogumentary
9. Shay Carl – ShayCarl
10. Paris Christou – ToonBoxStudio

JACKSGAP

▶ *"Hello there!"*

NAME:	Jack Harries
VLOGS AS:	JacksGap
DOB:	13/05/93
BORN:	London
VLOGGING SINCE:	2011
FIRST VID:	My First You Tube Video?
SUBSCRIBERS:	Over four million

Never thought I'd be...

- winning two Screenchart! Channel Awards for 'The Rickshaw Run'
- named (with Finn) as 'the hottest boys in the world' by *Tatler Magazine*
- offered shows on Sky TV and Capital Radio

Jack loves...

Bungee jumping, music (he calls it 'part of the creative process' and features a current playlist on his website), ball pits, fundraising for charities like The Teenage Cancer Trust.

Jack's vlog, which was born of a love of travel and a wish to document his pre-uni gap year, has come a long way since 2011! His brother Finn got involved three months' in – using his design and branding skills to send viewing figures shooting through the roof. Unusually however, this vlog's production values have been fantastic from the get-go. Jack's YouTube début was beautifully sharp and pacey, featuring clips within clips from a trip to Ibiza, plus a hilarious week long itinerary including waterskiing, an evening in the West End and a night in after being banned from his school prom. Jack's schedule is always packed. He might be skateboarding down a New York sidewalk, driving the width of India in a tuk-tuk for charity or just hanging in his room talking about who's the best twin. The boys attended the Harrodian school in Barnes before heading off to university – Jack to Bristol, Finn to Leeds. Both dropped out when it became obvious that working on JacksGap could afford them a living. The twins' parents are film producer Andy Harries and writer Rebecca Frayn.

> "WE'RE NOT PUTTING UP THE WALL THAT TV AND FILM HAVE. WE'RE JUST SAYING, "HEY, LOOK, CONNECT WITH US!"

CONNECT WITH JACK on...

Twitter @JacksGap and @JackHarries; instagram.com/jacksgap or via his website jacksgap.com

Wandering Vloggers

It's a great big world out there and who wouldn't want to see more of it? The vlogging trend can help whet your appetite for travel as you see places through the eyes of those passionate about what the planet has to offer.

Types of travel vlog include...

- **Gap year**
  After school and before uni, after uni and before your career – gap year vlogs really show you how to see the world without blowing the budget.

- **Lone wolf**
  Vlogs by solo travellers can inspire you to take the plunge to travel safely on your own, making friends and meeting locals along the way.

- **Extreme**
  Many travel vlogs show a destination experienced from a unique and thrilling perspective – think surfing in Nicaragua or paragliding in the Turkish hills.

The perfect travel vlog is...

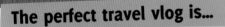

- **Authentic** – you need to have actually experienced the place you're talking about. If you've been somewhere but don't have live footage from the trip consider making a montage of your own photos with a voiceover.

- **Life-affirming** – a great travel vlog should make you want to seize the day and live life to the full on this wonderful planet.

- **Packed with locals** – talking to and spending time with local people before sharing their inside knowledge of a destination can really set your vlog apart.

At the Cole face

Travel vlogger Louis Cole from Cobham in Surrey has one amazing job, hot-desking around the world. The lucky guy spends his entire time travelling and documenting his adventures for his vlog, 'Fun For Louis'. He caught the travel bug as a kid thanks to his family's annual camping road trip to the south of France, which he says helped him "embrace journeying as a big part of holidays". As an adult he decided that he wanted "to take leave of predictable routines... be a nomad, a global citizen" and get out to celebrate life. With over a million subscribers he travels for free, financing his trips through a combination of sponsorship and on-site advertising revenue.

Too young to travel?

There are some seriously youthful vloggers out there, including sixteen-year-old New Yorker, Booker Mitchell. Booker travelled a lot with his parents and began a blog called 'Kids Travel' before starting his successful vlog, 'Booker Travels'. If you're not yet in a position to plan a gap year or fund your own travels, don't panic! It's never too soon to begin filming fun-packed day trips, weekends away or your annual summer holiday. Just make sure you let the sights, sounds and colours of the destination take centre stage.

TEN GREAT TRAVEL VLOGS

1. Jack and Finn Harries – JacksGap
2. Louis Cole – FunForLouis
3. Nadine Skyora – Hey Nadine
4. Booker Mitchell – Booker Travels
5. Sonia Gil – Sonia's Travels
6. Cailin O'Neil – Travel Yourself
7. Grant Schuman – Choose My Adventure
8. Rob Lloyd – Stop Having A Boring Life
9. Kate Thomas – TravelWithKate
10. Ben Brown – Mr Ben Brown

BRILLIANT BACKDROPS

As amazing as you are, it's not just you that needs to create a great impression with your viewer – your setting does, too. If you're out and about the view may do the work for you, but many posts are likely to be filmed in the comfort of your own home. If that's the case, don't sit in front of a pile of dirty laundry, half-eaten snacks or your unmade bed! Your surroundings should reflect the tone of your vlog, or, at the very least, not be needlessly distracting. Here's how to create a stunning setting.

Solid wall

Sit in front of a flat backdrop – plain white or magnolia isn't that inspiring, but a vibrant colour looks great. Avoid sitting directly in front of fussy wallpapers.

Room décor

If you can find an uncluttered room with warm woods and natural textures, this will hit the right note.

DIY colourama

If you can't afford a photographic colourama (who has the room for one anyway?), make your own backdrop. Buy a cheap clothes rail and some offcut cloth. Secure one end of the fabric over the rail so that it drapes to the floor. Pin it in place. Voilà! One backdrop, ready to go.

Soft and twinkly

Strings of warm white fairy lights strung up across a backdrop, above a mirror or draped around a bed head create a cosy feel and lovely ambient lighting for your shoot.

Outdoors

Vlogs from the great outdoors offer interest and variety. Find somewhere that is well lit, but avoid filming with direct sunlight shining unflatteringly on your face. Show off the scenery, but make sure you don't jerk the camera too fast as you pan round.

Remember – as you evolve, your backdrop will too. These YouTubers' settings are a million miles away from the ones they filmed in the beginning:

Zoella

Zoella's childhood room was cute… but no match for her twinkly new crib.

Miranda Sings

Miranda couldn't even be bothered to shut her closet in her dingy room!
Now she appears in front of a wall of fan art.

CharlieIsSoCoolLike

It's not just Charlie who's cleaned up his act…

Jim Chapman

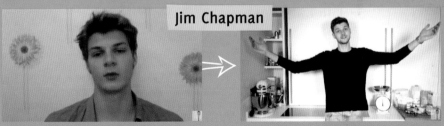

It's wallpaper, Jim – but not as we know it! Nowadays Jim is cooking on gas!

Beauty by Brandy

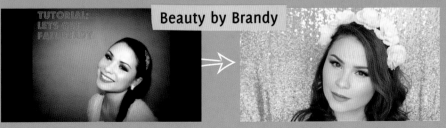

Brandy was shady, but now she's sparkly and gorgeous.

Furry Friends

We love animals, and we sure do love watching them online! Funny, wild and clever creature clips are all over the Internet – from cute kitties to funny bunnies, waving whales and loving lions. Here is our pick of the best.

Wild encounters

Tourists on safari filmed this epic battle between crocodiles, lions and a herd of buffalo at Kruger National Park in South Africa.

This driver has a lucky escape from a charging rhino.

Who knew seals were such keen surfers?

Oscar®-worthy performances

Beware the mutant giant spider dog – AKA Chica. She currently has over 140 million views.

Move over Jay Z, it's cat-lover-turned-rapper Cory William's Mean Kitty Song about mischievous puss, Sparta.

This cat sure can play. Forty million of us have watched him.

Should I put my pet online?

Cruelty to animals is most definitely not funny or clever. You should never do anything that would put your pet in danger or cause them unnecessary stress. However, filming your dog or cat's natural behaviour is fine. So, if your cat is always falling asleep and toppling off the window sill, or your dog howls in time to music, or your pet is just super, super cute, get filming! If you're a real animal lover, why not start a vlog about your pets, showing how you care for and play with them?

Heartwarming tales

Christian the lion, now totally wild and head of a pride, is reunited with the two people who looked after him as a cub. The footage will bring you to tears.

A family's feline rushes to the rescue! Cat Tara saves her owner, Jeremy, from being bitten by a stray dog.

Funny moments

Aaatchoo! This sneezing baby panda has amassed an astonishing 100 million views.

Fenton! When a guy took his Labrador, Fenton, for a walk in Richmond Park, he should have kept him on the lead. This clip of dog chasing deer has been viewed over 12 million times.

Q: Which dog is known on YouTube as 'The World's Cutest Dog Ever!'

Turn to page 96 to see the answer.

UNBOX CLEVER

A vlog doesn't have to be complicated to be hugely successful and financially lucrative. Some of the biggest clips on the net feature people opening up packages! Welcome to the world of unboxing...

Types of unboxing vlog include...

- **Toys**
  The most popular type of unboxing videos offer the same thrills as a look under the tree on Christmas morning.

- **Trainers**
  Sportswear in general is a massive theme.

- **Tech**
  From phones to games consoles to TVs, these are as appealing for adults as they are for teens.

Slice of Evan

When Evan was five years old he and his dad Jared began making short stop-motion animated videos using clay Angry Birds models. Evan asked his dad to upload the clips to YouTube so his friends could see them. When one of his videos amassed over a million views Jared realised that there might be more to Evan's videos than they had imagined. Since then his channel EvanTubeHD has gone from strength to strength. Occasionally his sister Jillian or his parents feature in the clips, but the real charm is watching a young boy enjoying different toys. Evan is rumoured to make a million dollars a year from his channel, but the money is all being banked to fund a college education for him and his sister.

The perfect unboxing vlog is...

- **Soothing** – calming voiceovers explain and explore all the elements of the item being unboxed.

- **Artistic** – great toy unboxers often create content based on stop frame animation using the toy figures they unwrap.

- **Packed with demos** – its not enough to just see the item, we want to see it in action.

Why do kids love unboxing?

It's hard to see the appeal of the unboxing trend, but it's a true YouTube obsession. Tracey of MG Tracey, a UK channel says "Children of all ages and all languages love watching surprise opening and unboxing videos. They sometimes watch them over and over again. Their feedback shows us they get the same sort of excitement watching us open toys, as they do opening their own gifts on birthdays and Christmas."

TEN GREAT TOY UNBOXING VLOGS

1. FunToyzCollector – the biggest unboxer on the net. Fans love her cool nail art and soothing voice.
2. Toys And Funny Kids Surprise Eggs – no voiceovers and fun music give mass appeal.
3. Kids Toys – hosted by two girls who open and play with the toys.
4. Evan Tube HD – hosted by Evan and sister Jillian. Features shot of item and great reviews.
5. Baby Big Mouth – as well as unboxing, this tries to teach simple concepts to kids.
6. Surprise Eggs Unboxing Toys – heavy on Playdoh.
7. Surprise Toys – opens a vast amount of surprise eggs.
8. Disney Car Toys – co-hosted by Sandy and Spiderman, uploads two to three vids a day.
9. Blu Toys – focusses on surprise eggs and features titles in multiple languages.
10. Kitties Mama – siblings Noah, Jonah and Emma host.

INTRODUCING

JENN IM

▶ "Welcome back..."

NAME:	Jenn Im
VLOGS AS:	Clothes Encounters
DOB:	22/03/89
BORN:	Los Angeles, USA
VLOGGING SINCE:	2010
FIRST VID:	Summer Fashion Haul with best friend Sarah
SUBSCRIBERS:	Over a million

Never thought I'd be...

- making a comfortable career out of my hobby of styling and self-expression
- be flown out to New York Fashion Week
- showing journalists around my apartment

Jen loves...

Hot Cheetos crisps, coffee, the 'shuffle' option on Spotify, heeled boots, steamed broccoli (she eats it daily for breakfast), being shot from below (she's very small).

Clothes Encounters' vlogger Jenn Im has got to be one of the sweetest people on YouTube. Her pet hate is having so little time with fans at 'assembly line meet and greets.' Instead she wishes she could go for dinner with small groups at a time so she could remember all of their faces and stories. With over a million subscribers to her channel this would be, as she says, 'a lot of dinner parties'! Effervescent, pretty and totally non-judgemental, Jenn is a breath of fresh air. The Korean/American has a cool take on fashion mistakes, believing that it's all about having fun. "Fashion is a form of art, a way you express yourself," she says. "Trends come and go, chances are you're going to look at a picture of you five years ago and think 'what the hell was I wearing?', but we're all going to think that." Jenn started her vlog because she wanted to combine her loves of fashion and video editing. She is adored for her personal style and great fashion tips.

> "I CONSIDER EACH ONE OF YOU GUYS WATCHING AS PART OF ME. YOU'VE HELPED ME SO MUCH WITH MY CONFIDENCE AND MY LIFE. SO THANK YOU."

CONNECT WITH JENN on...

Twitter @imjennim; instagram.com/imjennim or via Facebook/theclothesencounters

Fashionistas in the Frow

You don't have to be strutting the catwalk to walk with the fash pack. Vloggers around the world are showing off their style in so many ways! Just go online to pick up style notes, unpick new trends and watch stars walking you through their wardrobes.

Types of fashion vlog include...

- **Get ready with me**
  Full styling video for a night out or an event like a prom, that shows you how to create a look from top to toe.

- **Look books**
  A homemade live action photoshoot, featuring the vlogger wearing various outfits. Each item is name-checked for its label and sometimes price.

- **Outfit diaries**
  Often posted by month or season, these are a fly-on-the-wall slice of a vlogger's life. They include nights out, holidays and beach trips – always with style in mind.

The perfect fashion vlog is...

- **360°** – the vlogger shows each outfit from every angle and with close-ups.

- **Aspirational** – the perfect fashion vlog should whet your appetite for key pieces and leave you excited to create your own look.

- **Thrifty** – we want to look good without blowing the budget! A great fashion vlog shows you how to, using charity or vintage shops, update and upcycle your wardrobe.

Natasha knows how

Successful model, blogger and vlogger Natasha Ndlovu may have gorgeous looks and a great figure, but she's more than just a pretty face. Now living in west London, Natasha has a degree in visual arts. She's also a talented linguist speaking English, French, Spanish, Ndebele and Russian. Natasha first began her blog in 2013, turning to vlogging in 2014. Her 'How to...' videos, showing how to work tricky looks like double denim and head to toe white, are super popular.

Frow *Adjective-Noun [Abbreviation]*
Abbreviation of the words 'front' and 'row' at a fashion show.

What if I don't get invited to fashion shows?

The fashion industry has finally woken up to the power and influence of vloggers on consumers, so the top stars do get invited to major shows these days. However, you don't have to be in the front row of LFW to create great content, you just need to have a passion for fashion. Take tips from the competition and watch how others make their mark, then create your own channel around your particular style.

Look 4
Indian Fire
dress from eBay

TEN GREAT FASHION VLOGS

1. Jenn Im – Clothes Encounters
2. Anastasjia Louise Miller – Anastasjia Louise
3. Shirley Eniang – Shirley B. Eniang
4. Amy Spencer – The Little Magpie
5. Natasha Ndlovu – Bisous Natasha
6. Jessie – SunbeamsJess
7. Marzia Bisognin – Cutie Pie Marzia
8. Victoria Magrath – InTheFrow
9. Rhiannon – Fashion Rocks My Socks
10. Olivia Purvis – What Olivia Did

Let's Get Serious

$E = MC$

If you're not into shopping, showbiz or showing off your gaming skills, you might be looking to view something more meaty and meaningful in your online viewing. Never fear! Vlogs aren't all about performing crazy food challenges and organizing the contents of your bathroom cabinets. There are plenty of people posting interesting and educational content in a fun, original way.

Types of serious vlog include...

- **Science**
  Physics, chemistry, biology and even archaeology – you'll find a science vlog to explain everything you ever wanted to know.

- **Maths**
  What's not to love about a vlog that makes maths easier to understand?

- **English, history, politics and more...**
  Prefer art and literature? There's plenty to choose from online!

The perfect edu-vlog is...

- **Visual** – fun graphics and hands-on experiments help the viewer understand and digest even the most complex fact.

- **Funny** – geek humour is the best!

- **Helpful** – lots of take-home value for the viewer.

Dianna Cowern AKA Physics Girl

This girl could be the reason you ace your next science test! Dianna epitomizes why you should never judge a book by its cover. With her blonde hair and pretty face, she wouldn't be out of place on the front of a fashion magazine. Instead Dianna is on a one-girl mission to bring science to the masses with her enthusiastic, sunny presenting style and fascinating content. She vlogs on the physics behind everyday phenomena like rainbows, posts great interviews with eminent scientists, tests out and explain strange occurrences and even gives you experiments to try. Her sign-off is 'Happy Physicsing!'

John Green of SciShow and CrashCourse vlogs is a famous author. Unscrabble the letters to discover three of his brilliant books…

A Tearful Shin Tutors   _ _ _ / _ _ _ _ _ _ / _ _ / _ _ _ / _ _ _ _ _

Rap Not Pews   _ _ _ _ _ / _ _ _ _ _

Kangaroo Flak Soil   _ _ _ _ _ _ _ _ / _ _ _ / _ _ _ _ _ _

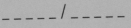

TEN GREAT EDUCATIONAL VLOGS

1. Dianna Cowern – Physics Girl
2. Charlie McDonnell – CharlieIsSoCoolLike
3. Sanne Vliegenthart – BooksAndQuills
4. Carrie Anne Philbin – GeekGurlDiaries
5. Derek Muller – Veritasium
6. Victoria Hart – ViHart
7. Hank and John Green – CrashCourse
8. Hank and John Green – SciShow
9. Brady Haran – NumberPhile
10. Jake McGowan-Lowe – Jakes Bones

IT'S WAY PAST MY BEDTIME

▶ "*Afternoon!*"

NAME:	Carrie Hope Fletcher
VLOGS AS:	It's Way Past My Bedtime
DOB:	22/10/82
BORN:	Harrow, London
VLOGGING SINCE:	2011
FIRST VID:	The Only Exception Cover
SUBSCRIBERS:	Over half a million

Never thought I'd be...

- author of my own self-help book for teens *All I Know Now*
- corresponding via video posts with my brother Tom and his wife Giovanna
- hobnobbing on the red carpet at film premières

Carrie loves...

Drinking tea, actress Emma Thompson, *Doctor Who* (she'd loved to play his assistant), haggis, *Tangled* and other Disney films, singing show tunes, playing guitar, ukulele and piano.

Carrie Fletcher is nothing short of a phenomenon. The sister of McFly and McBusted front man Tom Fletcher, her showbiz career began when she was spotted picking her brother up from his stage school. It soon became clear that like Tom, Carrie was immensely talented. She quickly found her way into the West End, starring in musicals like *Chitty Chitty Bang Bang* and *Les Misérables*. She is the only actress ever to have played the parts of Eponine as both a child and an adult. Carrie began vlogging in 2011, uploading clips of herself playing guitar and singing cover versions, but as she found her stride and gained followers she began talking about issues affecting teenage girls. This year her first book was published – a self-help title called *All I Know Now: Wonderings And Reflections On Growing Up Gracefully*.

> "SOCIAL MEDIA IS ALL ABOUT PRESENTING THE HAPPIEST, MOST POSITIVE VERSION OF YOURSELF TO THE WORLD. I'M HERE TO SAY THAT WE ALL HAVE BAD DAYS AND THAT IT'S EASY TO FEEL ISOLATED."

CONNECT WITH CARRIE on...

Twitter @CarrieHFletcher; instagram.com/carriehopefletcher or via her website carriehopefletcher.com

SHOWBIZ VLOGS

Sometimes the vlog comes after the fame. There are plenty of celebs who despite being huge names in other areas of media, also want a slice of the digital pie.

Types of showbiz vlog include...

- **Confessional**
  Nowadays stars use this platform to talk intimately about an issue, directly to their fans, rather than via the press.

- **VEVO**
  The go-to vlog channel for the music industry stars.

- **Blooper**
  Celebs love us to know they make mistakes, too. Many post outtakes which didn't make the final vlog post.

The perfect showbiz vlog is...

- **A-list** – the bigger the star reaching out via this new platform, the better.

- **Revelatory** – we want to see more, hear more, know more, about the star vlogger.

- **Conversational** – we love to feel like we're chatting with a friend... who just happens to be a huge star.

Ashley Tisdale

Ashley is a former Disney Channel staple and star of the *High School Musical* franchise, but she's not too high and mighty to share her life with us. Her vlogs are fun, glamorous and varied, including backstage clips, music videos, challenges and web-cam chats. Fans can watch Ash detailing her worst break-up experience, grabbing snacks from a convenience store in her PJs and auditioning the band for her new album.

Q: Which former Disney star is Demi Lovato's on-off friend and vlogging buddy?

Check your answer on page 96.

Why do celebrities want to vlog?

It's not about needing the money, but celebrities like (let's face it, need) to stay in the public eye. By vlogging they get to retain full creative autonomy – meaning they don't have a director or producer telling what they can and can't say. They can also film from the comfort of their own home without having to brave the paparazzi outside the front door. Finally, it's a way of properly connecting with fans and getting real and instant feedback.

3

5

10

TEN GREAT STAR VLOGS

1. Rainn Wilson – Soul Pancake
2. Ashley Tisdale – Ashley Tisdale
3. Jim Carrey – JimCarreyTruLife.com
4. Lo Bosworth – Lo Bosworth
5. Miley Cyrus – Miley Cyrus
6. Maddie Ziegler – Maddie Ziegler
7. Russell Brand – Russell Brand
8. Tom Fletcher – Tom Fletcher
9. John Green – Vlogbros
10. Demi Lovato – Demi Lovato

Me And The

Music

It all started with Justin Bieber. Way before his bad boy days, Biebz was a YouTube sensation, uploading videos of himself crooning to his guitar in his bedroom. Viewers soon cottoned on to his raw talent. Justin's YouTube videos were directly responsible for bringing him to the attention of manager Scooter Braun, who guided him to fame and fortune.

Nowadays YouTube is seen as the perfect portal and platform to showcase musical talent. Aussie band Five Seconds Of Summer formed on the back of lead singer Luke Hemmings' video clips. Singers Cody Simpson and Austin Mahone both became Internet sensations before snagging record deals. If you're musically minded, don't hide your light under a bushel! Grab your guitar, move over to the mic and press record.

It happened for them...

Ria Ritchie

After recording acoustic covers and uploading them to YouTube, Ria Ritchie was spotted by UK artist Plan B, who is now producing her first album.

Greyson Chance

Chat show host Ellen Degeneres was so impressed when she saw Greyson Chance online that she made him the first signed artist to her own record label.

These faces all found fame through YouTube – can you ID them? The answers are on page 96!

1. ....

2. ....

3. ....

4. ....

5. ....

Ten Great Young YouTube Singers

1. Johnny Orlando – Johnny Orlando
2. Angela Vazquez – Vazquez Sounds
3. Carson Lueders – Carson Lueders
4. Jordyn Jones – Jordyn Jones
5. Alex Buonopane – Alex B
6. Madeleine Jane Gray – MaddiJaneMusic
7. Manu Rios – Manu Rios
8. Jannina Weigel – Jannina W
9. Griffin Tucker – Griffin Tucker
10. Jasmine Thompson – Jasmine Thompson

CASPAR LEE

▶ _"Hi, my name is Caspar Lee."_

PRANK!

NAME:	Caspar Richard Lee
VLOGS AS:	dicasp
DOB:	24/04/94
BORN:	Paddington, London
VLOGGING SINCE:	2010
FIRST VID:	No longer available – it featured Caspar in the bath
SUBSCRIBERS:	Over four million

Never thought I'd be...

- nominated for UK's Favourite Vlogger in the 2015 Nickelodeon Kid's Choice Awards
- landing the part of Seagull Number Two in *The Spongebob Movie: Sponge Out Of Water* and Garlic in *Spud 3*.
- Starring in Style Haul series, *The Crew*.

Caspar loves...

Sleeping, all time bezzie Josh (the pair met at high school), winning at tennis, family (including his mum and sis Theodora Lee), milkshakes and pizza.

Caspar Lee is kidding his way through life! Born in London, he grew up in South Africa. As a fourteen-year-old working on a school project, Caspar became interested in creating video content. It wasn't until September 2010 however, that he posted his first clip on YouTube. He quickly gained a following, but when his account was hacked had to start again from scratch. Luckily Caspar is a resilient type. Rather than letting this get him down, he used everything he'd learned from early experiences to come back stronger. In January 2012 he launched his new channel, immersing himself in the vlogging community and creating great content based on his talent for humour and love of pranking. With support from other successful YouTubers, particularly Jack Harries, it became huge. Caspar remains humble and thankful for his success –that's why we love him.

"I'M THE HAPPIEST I'VE EVER BEEN IN MY LIFE. I'M LITERALLY LIVING THE DREAM AND I BELIEVE IT'S ONLY THE BEGINNING."

CONNECT WITH CASPAR on...

Twitter @Caspar_Lee; instagram.com/caspar_lee or at www.facebook.com/casplee

JUST KIDDING

Who would have thought you could create a full time job from winding your mates up, and generally having fun at their expense? Believe it or not, this is an option. If you're a born pranker, read on to ensure your vlog gets laughs from everyone involved.

Types of prank vlog include...

- **Prank calls**
  All you need is a phone and a plan! YouTubers love to prank call each other, their parents or total strangers.

- **Scary pranks**
  From jumping out of cupboards, scary masks or creating 'bumps in the night', the possibilities to freak people out are endless.

- **Prop pranks**
  Trick dog poos, huge plastic booties, fake snakes and terrifying toy tarantulas – a prank is always better with a cool prop.

The perfect prank vlog is...

- **Nailed on the first take** – if your prank doesn't work the first time or you don't catch the result on film, don't try doing it again. Pranks are only funny when the reactions are genuine.

- **Cheeky** – the tone should be mischievous and mildly annoying, rather than unkind.

- **Safe** – a true prank should never, EVER put anyone in danger.

Joe-nly joking!

It would be tempting to dismiss Joe Sugg as just riding on the coat tails of his super-famous older sister, Zoe. But ThatcherJoe (after his former career as a roof thatcher), was born to vlog and his success is well deserved. Besides his hilarious pranks – often on roommate Caspar Lee, Joe is known for his awesome impressions. Mega fame beckons with Joe starring as seagull 'Kyle' in the latest SpongeBob movie and bagging a meeting with Simon Cowell to talk about Syco's digital project, 'YouGeneration'.

Q: Joe Sugg famously pranked Caspar Lee by filling his bedroom with what? He added extra shock factor by hiding Oli White in the middle of the room, dressed in which outfit? Flip to page 96 for the answers!

Is there such a thing as crossing the line?

There is a fine line between pranking and bullying. To keep yourself firmly on the funny and friendly side, ask yourself the following: Firstly, 'does my prank put anyone at risk of harm?'. If the answer is 'yes', rethink. Secondly, 'who is laughing here?'. If the prank is designed to make a person feel humiliated, it's not a prank. Thirdly, ask 'am I out for revenge?'. Playing a revenge prank on a fellow joker is fine, but don't do it out of the blue to redress another grievance.

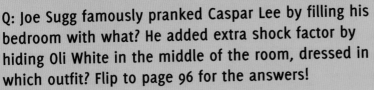

TEN GREAT PRANKING VLOGS

1. Casper Lee – DiCasp
2. Joe Sugg – ThatcherJoe
3. Jesse Wellens and Jeanna Smith – PrankvsPrank and BFvsGF
4. Remi Gaillard – NQTV
5. Rahat Hossain – MagicOfRahat
6. Pierre Girard and Jacques Chevalier – Just For Laughs Gags
7. Charlie Todd – Improv Everywhere
8. Robert Hoffman – PunchRober
9. Ed Bassmaster – Ed Bassmaster
10. Roman Atwood – RomanAtwoodVlogs

Up Close and

Nice to meet you!

Hi there!

PERSONAL

Although you don't want to be a crazy stalker person, it's nice to see your favourite vloggers in the flesh. Here are some of the ways you can get up close and personal with your online idols...

Brighton, East Sussex

Brighton is a mecca for vloggers. Lots of stars, including Zoella and PewDiePie, are based there, loving the cosmopolitan flavour of the English seaside town. Zoella has been spotted sipping hot chocolate in The Marwood, a coffee shop on Ship Street in the Lanes, while Pewds and girlfriend Marzia love browsing the shops and walking along the seafront. Alfie Deyes can't say enough about what the place has to offer, "There's street art, cool-looking buildings, individual shops and not just big brands everywhere. There's a real sense of community." Of course you may not run into these guys or any other star vloggers if you go to Brighton, but we can guarantee you'll have a great day out. Be sure to visit the pier and the Royal Pavilion!

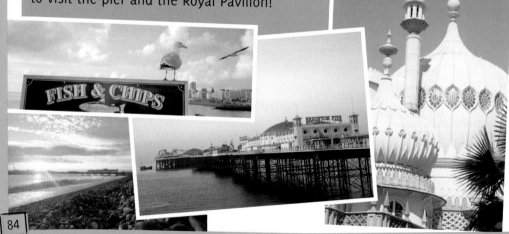

London Fashion Week

LFW is a global highlight on the international fashion calendar – no self-respecting fashion or style vlogger would miss it. Even if you can't get tickets for the shows there are various panel and insider events every year. Visit sites like Topshop, ASOS and Ticketmaster to check out what's being planned. Even if you're too late for the events it's worth indulging in some people spotting around the venues, as well as visiting any free exhibits open to the general public.

Q: How many famous faces can you identify on the front row at Julien Macdonald's Show during London Fashion Week? Check your answer on page 96.

Book launches

So many vloggers are turning into authors! Book launches and in-store signings are another way to show you're a true fan. Stars will often go on nationwide tours, so you may even discover that they are appearing at a bookshop near you. Events like these are always a bit manic as people camp out and queue for hours, so be prepared to wait your turn. Visit your favourite vlogger's channel, Twitter feed or publisher's page to check for details of forthcoming launches.

TV appearances

Zoella and her friends are becoming such big names they're even being invited onto mainstream television. Zoella has appeared on ITV show *Loose Women* and Alfie Deyes has been interviewed on the *BBC Breakfast* show. Many vloggers tweet details of the shows they are planning to film – giving you time to get audience tickets.

Digital events

If you're prepared to travel and don't mind huge crowds of people, annual digital events offer another opportunity to engage with your fave vlogging stars. Here you can expect to mingle with like-minded fans of new media, listen to talks and even grab a selfie with the stars themselves at meet and greets. Gatherings are held all over the world, so it's just a case of picking something local. Think about...

SUMMER IN THE CITY – EXCEL, LONDON
VISIT WWW.SITC-EVENT.CO.UK

VIDFESTUK – EXCEL, LONDON.
VISIT WWW.MCMCOMICCON.COM

AMITYFEST – BRIGHTON DOME
VISIT WWW.TWITTER.COM/AMITYFEST

VIDCON – ANAHEIM, CALIFORNIA
VISIT WWW.VIDCON.COM

CHANGING TIMES

The world of vlogging is constantly changing – you've got to work hard to keep your finger on the pulse! Check out the channels of these up-and-coming vlogging stars and then test yourself on the latest scoops.

Lia Marie Johnson

Hawaiian-born Lia has been posting clips online for years. Now she is a breakthrough Internet star. Her channel showcases her musical talents, alongside challenges and memes. Check out her wicked Miley Cyrus *Can't Stop* parody!

Emily Jade

Emily is known for her fun, lively clips, filmed mostly in her room. Many also feature her little sister and her BFFs. Emily has been picked up by YouTube teen partner collab SevenSuperGirls.

Zay Zay and Jo Jo

Isaiah Fredericks is the son of US comedian Kevin and has his own channel, ZayZayFredericks, also featuring his younger brother.

Jenn McAllister

Inspired by watching Smosh, Jenn McAllister began her channel JennXPenn in the summer holidays between school years six and seven. She was soon snapped up to be part of YouTube's teen empire AwesomenessTV and now boasts two million subscribers, a clutch of award nominations, her first book deal and movie role in *Bad Night*.

Charisma Kain

San Diego teen Charisma rose to web stardom with the band Pink Army. She continues to post regularly. As well as having amazing musical skills, Charisma also appears on Nickelodeon's *AwesomenessTV*.

Jake Mitchell

The hottie from Herefordshire began vlogging in 2013 and now has a huge online following. He has played in celebrity football tournament, Soccer Six, and also presents *Technobabble* on CBBC.

HERE IS THE NEWS

Can you ace this news-based quiz? Give it a try, then check your answers on page 96.

1. Which pair of YouTube stars recently announced that they had their own waxworks at Madame Tussauds?

2. What is Joe Sugg's debut graphic novel called?

3. Zoella won the UK Favourite Vlogger award at the Kid's Choice Awards in 2015, but three other vloggers were nominated. Can you name them?

4. Who is this British vlogger? Can you name his comedy partner?

5. Who did Jim Chapman say was the most inspirational woman he'd ever worked with at the 2015 Glamour Women of the Year Awards?

6. Tyler Oakley recently came under fire from pop fans for allegedly dissing which member of One Direction?

7. Which YouTuber recently scored a book deal for a funny self-help title?

8. Which band of singing songstresses have signed a digital, TV and film deal with Entertainment One?

WANNA **JOIN IN?**

Vlogging is fun, exciting and informative, and with enough time and energy in the long run it can even be lucrative. If you still need some golden nuggets of advice, get them from those in the know…

"My first bit of advice would be: try to use a half-decent camera if you can – a standard digital camera works well – and try to film in natural light from the window." – **Zoe Suggs/Zoella**

"Before diving into the world of stuff-making, you need to watch a lot of stuff. Discover what excites and inspires you and let it shape you as a creative… footnote, watch poorly made and unsuccessful content too and work out why it didn't work. Learn from others' mistakes." – **Thomas Ridgewell/Tomska**

"One of the most crucial parts to building a strong community is being consistent – not just by uploading frequently, but also by responding to comments. It's important to show your audience that you appreciate their support by always interacting with them." – **Bethany Mota**

"Don't think about success: Think about what you want to put out. Treat it like a hobby or passion project, and your authenticity will naturally shine through." – **Michelle Phan**

"You need to ask yourself what makes a channel good. In my opinion, it's the helpfulness and individual quirks of each guru. Think about it this way: why do you love your closest friends?" – **Cassandra Bankson/ DiamondsAndHeels14**

"Good things come to those who wait, so just remember that whenever you feel like smashing your head on your keyboard because you don't have all the followers you wish you had. Blogging should be fun, and an extension of you and the things you love. If it isn't fun, and you aren't enjoying it or getting any satisfaction out of it, maybe it's just not your scene." – **Anna Gardner/ViviannaDoesMakeup**

"Remember, sending annoying spam messages plugging your videos isn't the way to get attention for your channel. Instead, make video responses to others' videos and interact with people. Make friends."
– **Sanne Vliegenthart/BooksAndQuills**

"If you run into an issue with editing or filming, take initiative and find the answer online. Google is your best friend!" – **Jenn Im**

"Don't forget to be interesting – I even write out scripts sometimes to make sure what I'm saying isn't dull as hell... Do not be afraid to fail... Watch early VlogBrothers videos and see that we sucked too." – **Hank Green/VlogBrothers**

Use this page to explore your future as a vlogger. Finish the sentences and you will start to create a picture of the kind of person you are, what matters to you and what you enjoy doing. This information should help you come up with an idea for your vlog.

People say I am

I really enjoy

My favourite way to spend the weekend is

I feel most strongly about

My favourite vlogs are

These vlogs work well because

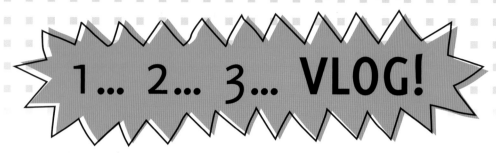

1... 2... 3... VLOG!

OK, so now you know what you want to vlog about, it's time to get started. Follow our step-by-step guide and you'll be onscreen before you can say, 'vlog it!'.

Step One – Choose a name

This needs to be short, simple and quirky, so that your audience can remember you and find you again. It also needs to be something that represents you and your brand. As so many domain names are already taken, consider a mash up of your name and a concept. Check that the name is free before you run with it – there are domain name checkers online.

Step Two – Create a YouTube channel

To do this you'll need to launch a web browser and visit YouTube. Click on the 'Sign In' link and then 'Create An Account'. You'll be prompted to create a new account. The Google username will become the name of your YouTube channel. Afterwards you can create your Google Account Profile and add a photo. You'll be directed back to sign into YouTube using your Google account username and password. From there go into the Google Account Menu, create your YouTube channel and edit your profile. Remember to check that it's okay with a parent or guardian.

Step Three – Practise and prepare

Getting comfortable in front of the camera takes time, so practise first. Make notes and rehearse in front of the mirror. Once you're ready, film some test footage and try speaking into the lens, not the viewing screen, so that you have direct eye contact with the viewer. Hone your voice (you'll need to speak slower and with more emphasis on pronunciation than you would normally). You may like to work from a script. This is fine, but don't read the lines on camera, as the recording should feel natural and spontaneous. Don't worry too much however, you can always edit your work.

Step Four – Set up

Follow the equipment checklist on the next page to ensure you have what you need to get started. Set up your filming location. If you're shooting indoors try putting a 'do not disturb' sign up to limit interruptions. Set up lighting and sound equipment, then get yourself into a comfortable position.

Step Five – Film

Record your content. As a rule it's better to have more rather than less footage. If you don't film it you won't be able to edit it, especially if you're into showing time-lapse footage of a process.

Step Six – Editing

Before you post your vlog make sure you know the basics of editing. This is an acquired skill and you'll improve as you go, but for the time being you should at least know how to jump cut. This will help you cut out mistakes and create a pacey, dynamic clip. Once you're happy, post the clip onto your channel.

Step Seven – Create a schedule

Consistency is vital in vlogging. Decide how often you plan to post clips, create a schedule and stick to it. The Internet is constantly changing and evolving so make sure you keep abreast of online and vlogging trends, adapting your content accordingly.

Step Eight – Network

Advertise your schedule to your followers within your channel and alert people to your presence by reacting to other's posts rather than spamming their channels with ads for yours. Find YouTubers at a similar subscriber level to you, like their clips and post positive comments about their content. Once you're up and running, think about collaborating with other YouTubers. This is a great way to increase your following.

Don't forget to have fun!

As many of the YouTubers have said, the most important thing is to enjoy what you're doing. Relax, be yourself and have fun!

VLOGGING **CHECKLIST**

☐ Camera

This could be an internal camera on a mobile phone or ideally a point and shoot device. If you're an active or sporty vlogger consider using a GoPro camera to capture your movement. Later down the line, you might even invest in a DSLR camera, which will give you the most professional picture quality.

☐ Microphone

Many devices have inbuilt microphones, which are fine. If you have a camera with an external microphone jack socket, then invest in an external directional mic. A cheap lapel mic works wonders, as does a camera mounted mic. If you don't have an external mic socket, record the video and sound simultaneously but separately using a program like Audacity. You will then need to import the audio and video from the camera to a video editing program and align them manually.

☐ Selfie stick

These are great if you're recording a vlog entry while you're out and about. You can clip your phone or camera in then get yourself and your background fully in-shot.

☐ Lighting

Where possible use natural light. Find a nice bright room, or sit near a window. If this isn't possible you still need to pay attention to the way your shot is lit. You can get a clear, bright setup that's flattering and professional by using anglepoise lamps and bouncing the light off pieces of white poster board (available at art shops). Once you're up and running and possibly earning money from your vlog, you can always invest in soft boxes that will diffuse the light and create an even look.

☐ Hardware and Software

A laptop computer is the best way to edit your material. You'll need some free editing software such as Windows Moviemaker or iMovie to get started. You can also use this to add titles and pictures. For animation you can use Animaker, then graduate to Adobe Flash. Resources like Audacity, Mixcraft or Dublt will allow you to add professional audio voiceovers and royalty-free soundtracks to cover up microphone hum.

Books by Greg James & Chris Smith

Kid Normal

Kid Normal and the Rogue Heroes

Kid Normal and the Shadow Machine

Kid Normal and the Final Five

And the World Book Day title

Kid Normal and the Loudest Library